IT'S TIME TO EAT PULASANS

It's Time to Eat PULASANS

Walter the Educator

Silent King Books
A WhichHead Entertainment Imprint

Copyright © 2025 by Walter the Educator

All rights reserved. No part of this book may be reproduced in any manner whatsoever without written per- mission except in the case of brief quotations embodied in critical articles and reviews.

First Printing, 2024

Disclaimer

This book is a literary work; the story is not about specific persons, locations, situations, and/or circumstances unless mentioned in a historical context. Any resemblance to real persons, locations, situations, and/or circumstances is coincidental. This book is for entertainment and informational purposes only. The author and publisher offer this information without warranties expressed or implied. No matter the grounds, neither the author nor the publisher will be accountable for any losses, injuries, or other damages caused by the reader's use of this book. The use of this book acknowledges an understanding and acceptance of this disclaimer.

It's Time to Eat PULASANS is a collectible early learning book by Walter the Educator suitable for all ages belonging to Walter the Educator's Time to Eat Book Series. Collect more books at WaltertheEducator.com

USE THE EXTRA SPACE TO TAKE NOTES AND DOCUMENT YOUR MEMORIES

PULASANS

Pulasan fruit, it's time to eat,

It's Time to Eat Pulasans

A jungle treat, so soft and sweet.

Its skin is red, with spikes so small,

A tasty treasure loved by all!

The tree stands tall, its branches wide,

The pulasans hang side by side.

We pick them ripe, their color bright,

They're ready now, such a delight!

We twist the fruit, it pops in two,

The juicy flesh comes into view.

It's soft and white, so sweet to see,

A hidden treat for you and me!

The seed inside is smooth and round,

It's tucked away, so safe and sound.

But all around, the fruit is there,

Its yummy flavor fills the air.

It's Time to Eat
Pulasans

It's juicy, soft, and oh, so fun,

A snack for all beneath the sun.

We take a bite, then laugh with glee,

Pulasan's joy is pure and free.

The taste is sweet, with just a snap,

It fills our hearts, no need to nap.

Its spiky shell may look so tough,

But peel it back, it's not so rough!

We share it round, with family near,

This tasty fruit brings lots of cheer.

The pulasan, both fun and rare,

A fruit that shows how much we care.

Let's thank the tree, so strong and true,

For giving us this fruit to chew.

Its branches hold this special prize,

It's Time to Eat
Pulasans

A gift beneath the tropic skies.

Eat it fresh or make a dish,

The pulasan's a perfect wish.

A treat for all, both big and small,

This little fruit can do it all!

So let's enjoy, and shout hooray,

The pulasan has made our day.

Its sweet, soft taste is such a treat,

It's Time to Eat
Pulasans

Pulasan time just can't be beat!

ABOUT THE CREATOR

Walter the Educator is one of the pseudonyms for Walter Anderson. Formally educated in Chemistry, Business, and Education, he is an educator, an author, a diverse entrepreneur, and he is the son of a disabled war veteran. "Walter the Educator" shares his time between educating and creating. He holds interests and owns several creative projects that entertain, enlighten, enhance, and educate, hoping to inspire and motivate you. Follow, find new works, and stay up to date with Walter the Educator™

at WaltertheEducator.com

www.ingramcontent.com/pod-product-compliance
Lightning Source LLC
LaVergne TN
LVHW052014060526
838201LV00059B/4028